# 1000
## *facts about*
# THE
# EARTH

MOIRA BUTTERFIELD

Kingfisher Books

NEW YORK

# Contents

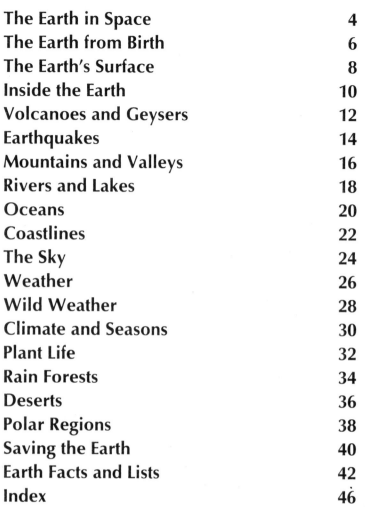

KINGFISHER
Larousse Kingfisher Chambers Inc.
95 Madison Avenue
New York, New York 10016

First American edition 1992
10 9 8 7 6 5

Produced by Times Four Publishing Ltd.
Designed by Margaret Howdle, Chris Leishman and Brian Robertson
Cover design by Terry Woodley
Additional text contributions by Catriona MacGregor
Consultant: Jill A. Wright
Illustrated by Mainline Design, Peter Bull, Sandy Hill
Printed in Spain

Library of Congress Cataloging-in-Publication Data
Butterfield, Moira,
The earth/Moira Butterfield; [illustrated by Mainline Design,
Peter Bull, Sandy Hill]. – 1st American ed.
p.   cm. – (1000 facts about)
Includes index.
Summary: Examines the volcanoes, rivers, deserts, rain forests,
weather, and other facets of our planet.
1. Earth–juvenile literature. [1. Earth–Miscellanea.]
I. Bull, Peter, 1960– ill. II. Hill, Sandy, ill. III. Mainline
Design (Firm) IV. Title. V. Series.
QB631.4.B88   1992
550–dc20      92-53101   CIP   AC
ISBN 1-85697-808-7

# Introduction

In this book you will be able to discover the most interesting and important facts about the Earth. First you can find out what kind of planet Earth is, and how scientists think it came to be formed. Then you can read about what the Earth is made of and how it has been shaped by earthquakes, volcanoes, rivers, and oceans. Find out, too, about the world's weather and the deserts, and other habitats that cover the surface.

Finally, you can read about the pollution that is threatening life on Earth, and about some of the things that are being done to save the wildlife and landscape.

To help you pick out the things you want to read about, some key words are in bold type like this: **volcano**.

Also, there are lots of easy-to-find facts beginning with a spot like this:

● Nearly all the birds that visit the Antarctic coast are seabirds.

Across the top of each page there are mini-facts, giving you useful lists — for example the world's most precious gems, or the names of the earliest creatures on Earth.

On each double-page there is a Strange but True box containing especially unusual or startling facts.

On pages 42–5 you will find charts and lists of Earth records and facts for you to refer to.

If you are not sure where to find facts about a particular topic, look in the Index on pages 46–8.

# The Earth in Space

Our world is a **planet** traveling through space. It journeys around a giant ball of fiery hot gases called the **Sun**.

The Sun is a **star**. It produces **light** and **heat** which reach the Earth.

The Earth is the only known planet that has **life** on it. It is ideal for living things because it has **water** and **air**.

## The Solar System

The Earth is part of the **Solar System**, a group of nine planets that travel through Space around the Sun.

- The Earth takes one year to travel around the Sun, a distance of 595 million miles (958 million km).

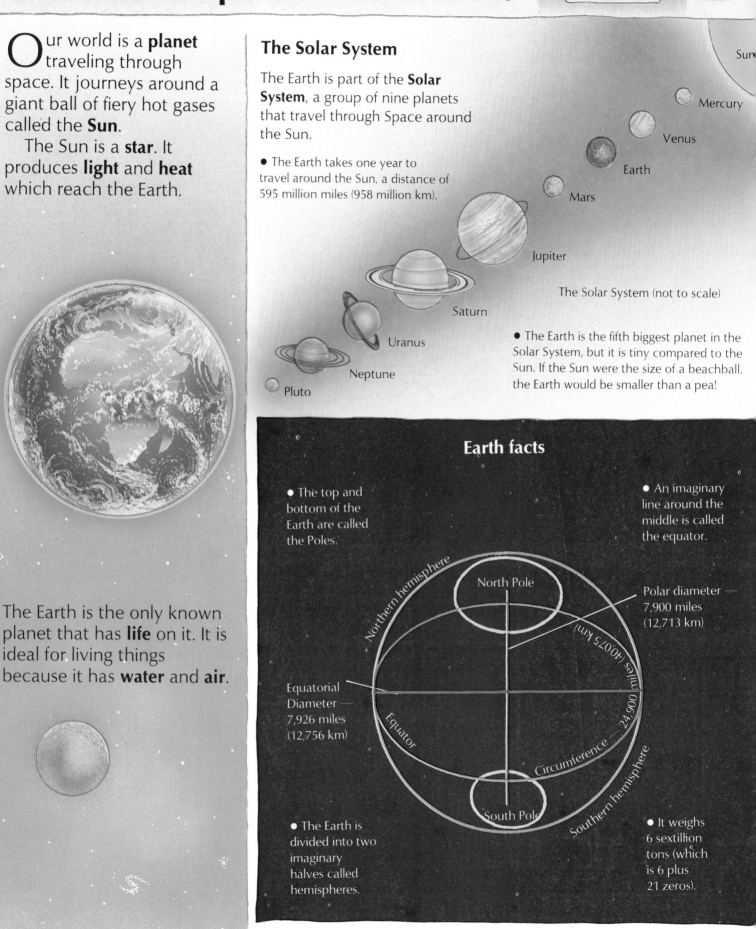

Sun

Mercury

Venus

Earth

Mars

Jupiter

The Solar System (not to scale)

Saturn

Uranus

Neptune

Pluto

- The Earth is the fifth biggest planet in the Solar System, but it is tiny compared to the Sun. If the Sun were the size of a beachball, the Earth would be smaller than a pea!

## Earth facts

- The top and bottom of the Earth are called the Poles.

- An imaginary line around the middle is called the equator.

Northern hemisphere

North Pole

Polar diameter — 7,900 miles (12,713 km)

Equatorial Diameter — 7,926 miles (12,756 km)

Equator

Circumference — 24,900 miles (40,075 km)

Southern hemisphere

South Pole

- The Earth is divided into two imaginary halves called hemispheres.

- It weighs 6 sextillion tons (which is 6 plus 21 zeros).

## Earth's orbit

The Earth's path around the Sun is called its **orbit**. It travels in a long oval shape called an **ellipse**. As it travels through space it spins around on its **axis**, an imaginary line through the center of the planet from Pole to Pole.

● The Earth spins on its axis once every 24 hours. When your part of the Earth turns away from the Sun, darkness falls.

● As the Earth travels around, your home begins to face the Sun again and daylight arrives.

● During the day, the Sun looks as if it is moving across the sky. In fact, it is the Earth that is moving, not the Sun.

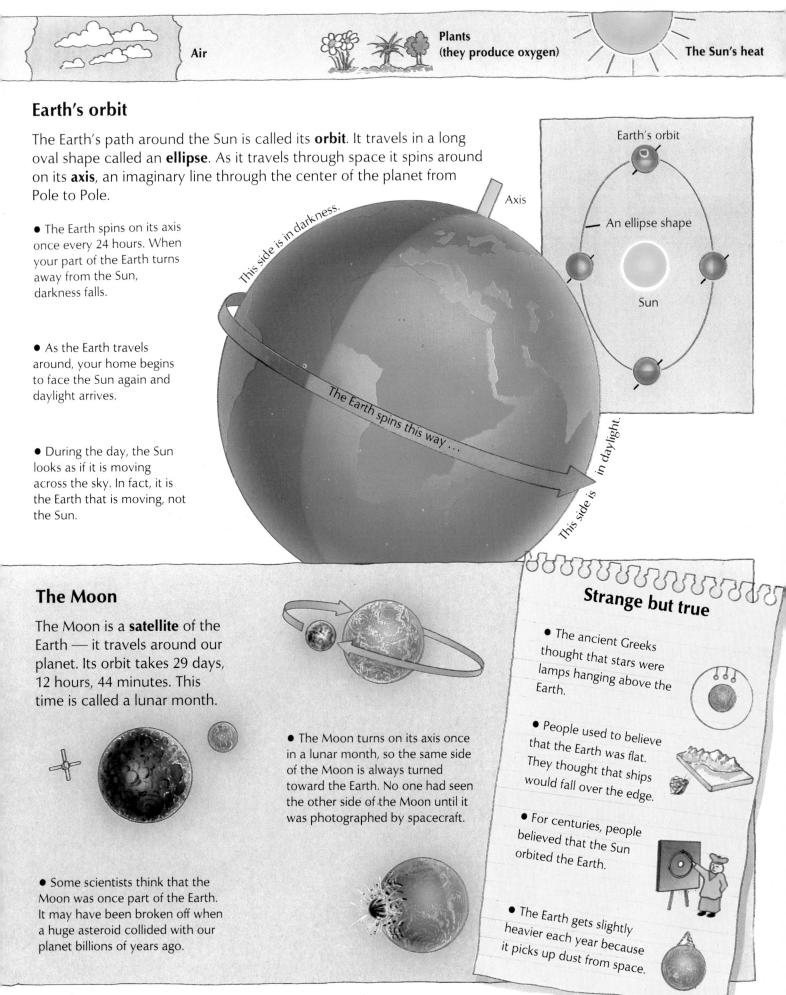

This side is in darkness.

Axis

The Earth spins this way ...

This side is in daylight.

Earth's orbit

An ellipse shape

Sun

## The Moon

The Moon is a **satellite** of the Earth — it travels around our planet. Its orbit takes 29 days, 12 hours, 44 minutes. This time is called a lunar month.

● The Moon turns on its axis once in a lunar month, so the same side of the Moon is always turned toward the Earth. No one had seen the other side of the Moon until it was photographed by spacecraft.

● Some scientists think that the Moon was once part of the Earth. It may have been broken off when a huge asteroid collided with our planet billions of years ago.

### Strange but true

● The ancient Greeks thought that stars were lamps hanging above the Earth.

● People used to believe that the Earth was flat. They thought that ships would fall over the edge.

● For centuries, people believed that the Sun orbited the Earth.

● The Earth gets slightly heavier each year because it picks up dust from space.

# The Earth from Birth

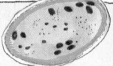

Blue-green algae

The Solar System was formed about **4.5 billion years** ago from a huge spinning cloud of gas and dust. The Sun was born at the center of the cloud.

Farther out, dust particles began to collect together as small lumps, which grew larger and larger as they collided. Eventually these became the **planets**, including the **Earth**.

The Earth started as a mass of red-hot rock. Around a billion years after it had formed, it was cool enough for oceans to form on the surface. These are where the first life forms developed.

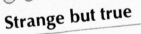

## Strange but true

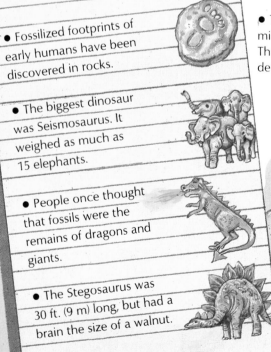

- Fossilized footprints of early humans have been discovered in rocks.

- The biggest dinosaur was Seismosaurus. It weighed as much as 15 elephants.

- People once thought that fossils were the remains of dragons and giants.

- The Stegosaurus was 30 ft. (9 m) long, but had a brain the size of a walnut.

## Earth's beginnings

The development of the Earth is divided into five lengths of time called **eras**. The first two eras, the **Archaean** and the **Proterozoic**, lasted for four billion years, which is almost **80 percent** of the Earth's history.

- During the Archaean Era, the Earth was born. Water and gases such as oxygen were formed. Very simple life forms appeared between 3.5 and 4 billion years ago.

- During the Proterozoic Era, from about 2.5 billion to 570 million years ago, the first animals appeared in the sea. They were simple animals without backbones, such as worms and jellyfish.

- The Paleozoic era lasted from about 570 million years ago to 245 million years ago. During this time the Earth was covered in swamps. Larger plants, fish, and amphibians appeared.

- The Mesozoic era lasted from about 245 million years ago to 65 million years ago. In this period many animals developed, including giant reptiles called dinosaurs. The first mammals and birds also appeared.

- The Cenozoic era began about 65 million years ago and is still going on. The plants and animals we know today developed during this time.

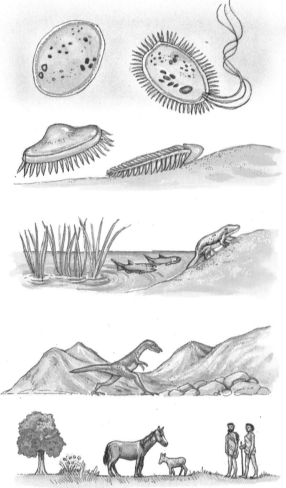

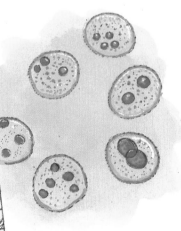

Microscopic plants called algae were amongst the first life forms.

## How life began

When the Earth was young, a mixture of different chemicals covered its surface. The Sun's radiation acted on the chemicals and they formed new materials called **amino acids** and **sugars**.

The amino acids and sugars linked up and eventually living **cells** were created. Cells are the smallest units of life, from which all living things are made.

Jellyfish  Spriggina worms  Dickinsonia worms  Sea pen corals

# Fossils

Scientists can tell what early plants and animals were like by looking at **fossils**. A fossil is the hardened remains or shape of an animal or plant preserved in rock.

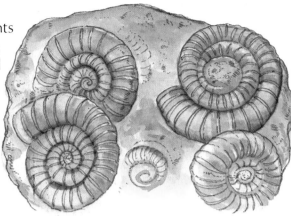

● A fossil forms when a dead animal or plant gets covered in mud or clay.

● The soft parts of the body decay, leaving the hard parts such as shell.

● Over thousands of years, the mud hardens into rock.

● Some animal and plant fossils have been found in pieces of amber, a fossilized resin which oozed from pine trees millions of years ago and then hardened.

Fossil in amber

● The oldest-known rocks were found in Greenland. They date from 3,800 million years ago.

Greenland

## Evolution

**Evolution** is the theory that animals and plants have gradually changed shape and form over millions of years, to enable them to survive in their surroundings. For instance, human beings probably evolved from apes.

# Dinosaurs

**Dinosaurs** were the biggest land animals that ever lived. They were reptiles with scaly skins.

● Plant-eating dinosaurs were huge. Brachiosaurus and Diplodocus were some of the biggest, up to 100 ft. (30 m) in length.

● Meat-eating dinosaurs were smaller and ran on hind legs. The largest was Tyrannosaurus, which stood about 16 ft. (5 m) tall.

The dinosaurs **disappeared** about 65 million years ago. No one knows exactly why. They may have died out because:

● An asteroid hit the Earth, throwing up so much dust that the Sun's rays were blocked out, leading to the death of plants and some of the biggest animals.

● The Earth's temperature heated up and became too warm for the dinosaurs.

● The mammal population grew bigger and took most of the dinosaurs' food.

# The Earth's Surface

Here are the seven continents:

Australia
3 million sq. miles
(7.7 million sq. km)

Asia
17 million
sq. miles
(44 million s

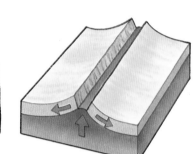

The Earth's outer shell is called the **crust**. It is divided into pieces called **plates**, which fit together rather like a jigsaw puzzle. They "float" on top of hot, partly molten rock (the **mantle**).

The crust forms the land and the ocean floor.

## The Earth's plates

The Earth's **plates** move around very, very slowly as they "float" on top of hot rock. As they move, they carry the land and the ocean floor with them. Sometimes the plates:

● Collide, pushing up mountains or creating deep ocean trenches and volcanoes (see p.12 and p.21).

● Slide slowly past each other, producing so much strain that they cause earthquakes (see p.14).

● Move apart so the ocean floor splits between them and molten rock rises up through cracks.

Plate

Plate

Floor spreads apart

Land

Ocean

Crust

Mantle

## Earth facts

● Greenland is the largest island in the world. It may possibly be several islands covered by a sheet of ice.

Greenland

● The northernmost point of land in the world is the islet of Oodaq near the North Pole. It is covered in ice.

● The southernmost point of land in the world is the Amundsen-Scott South Polar Station in Antarctica.

● The highest point of land in the world is Mount Everest in the Himalayan mountain range.

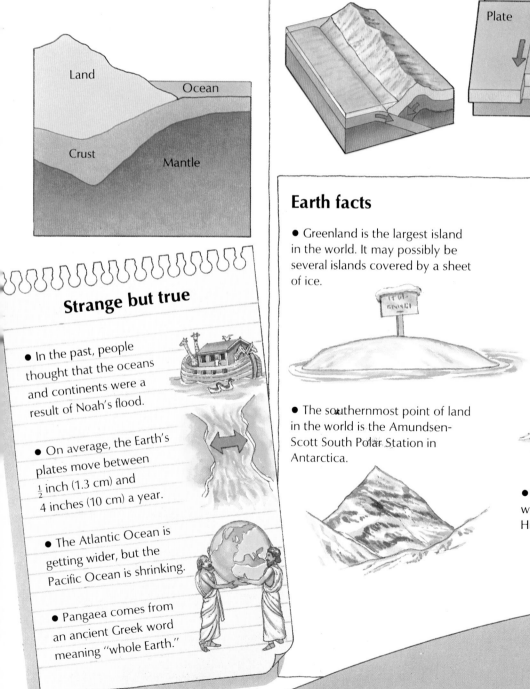

## Strange but true

● In the past, people thought that the oceans and continents were a result of Noah's flood.

● On average, the Earth's plates move between $\frac{1}{2}$ inch (1.3 cm) and 4 inches (10 cm) a year.

● The Atlantic Ocean is getting wider, but the Pacific Ocean is shrinking.

● Pangaea comes from an ancient Greek word meaning "whole Earth."

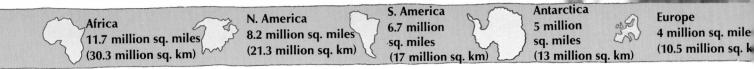

| Africa 11.7 million sq. miles (30.3 million sq. km) | N. America 8.2 million sq. miles (21.3 million sq. km) | S. America 6.7 million sq. miles (17 million sq. km) | Antarctica 5 million sq. miles (13 million sq. km) | Europe 4 million sq. mile (10.5 million sq. k |

# The continents

On maps, the land is divided into seven parts called **continents**. The continents are themselves moving, but very, very slowly — it has taken millions of years for them to reach where they are today.

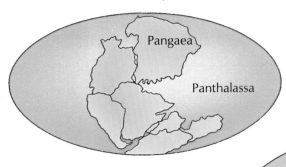

● About 120 million years ago there were two continents: Laurasia and Gondwanaland.

● Laurasia broke into North America, Europe, and Asia.

● The continents began as one big mass of land called Pangaea. It started to break up about 200 million years ago.

● Pangaea was surrounded by a single vast ocean called Panthalassa.

● Gondwanaland broke up to become Africa, South America, Antarctica, Australia, and India.

● The continents are still moving. For instance, North America moves away from Europe at a rate of about an inch (3 cm) a year.

# The past and the future

Here are some examples of the shape of continents in the **past**:

● The east coast of South America and the west coast of Africa were joined.

● The continents of Africa and Antarctica were also joined. There is proof of this because fossilized remains of tropical African plants and animals have been found in modern Antarctica.

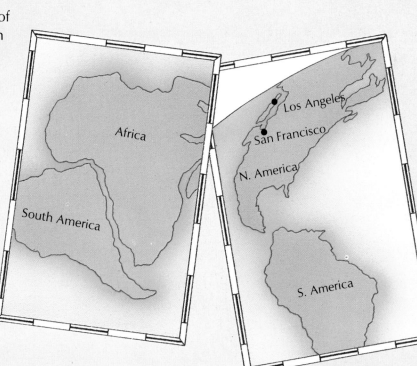

Here are some examples of what may occur in **50 million years** time:

● The two American continents will have broken apart.

● Africa and Asia will have broken apart.

● Part of California, including the city of Los Angeles, will have broken off from America.

# Inside the Earth

Here are the four most
precious gems to be
found on the Earth:

Ruby

The Earth is made up of four layers. The thin outer layer is called the **crust**. Then comes the hot, partly molten rock of the **mantle**.

Beneath the mantle there is a layer of liquid metal called the **outer core**.

In the center of the Earth, there is a ball of very hot solid metal called the **inner core**.

Crust
Mantle
Outer core
Inner core

## The Earth's layers

Scientists have worked out what is likely to be inside the Earth by analyzing **rocks** and by studying the **shock waves** that travel up to the surface during earthquakes (see pp.14/15).

- The Earth gets hotter toward its center. The temperature in the middle is thought to be more than 9,000°F (5,000°C).

- New crust is being made all the time, as molten rock bubbles up through huge cracks between plates in the ocean floor. (see p.12).

- There are two kinds of Earth crust — ocean crust beneath the seas and continental crust beneath the land.

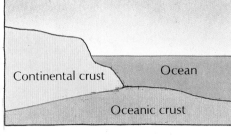

Continental crust    Ocean

Oceanic crust

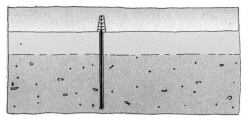

- The deepest rock samples ever gathered came from a hole drilled 60 miles (100 km) down from the surface.

## Strange but true

- Diamonds are harder than any other natural substance.

- Children playing on a beach made the first discovery of a South African diamond.

- The largest diamond ever found weighed over a pound (half a kilogram).

- Diamonds are made of the same substances as coal soot and other carbons.

## Rocks

There are three different types of rock on Earth. They are given the names **igneous**, **sedimentary**, and **metamorphic**.

- Igneous rocks are formed when hot molten material called magma bubbles up from beneath the crust and hardens.

- Metamorphic rocks are rocks that have been changed and hardened by heat and pressure. Limestone, for example, can change into marble.

- Some sedimentary rocks are made from pieces of older rocks which collect in layers, usually beneath the sea. As the layers pile up, the material is squeezed into rock — sand becomes sandstone, mud becomes clay.

- Other sedimentary rocks form from layers of dead animals and plants on the seabed.

Sedimentary rocks:
Sandstone
Limestone          Shale

Igneous rocks:
Pumice   Obsidian
     Granite

Metamorphic rocks:
Marble      Slate

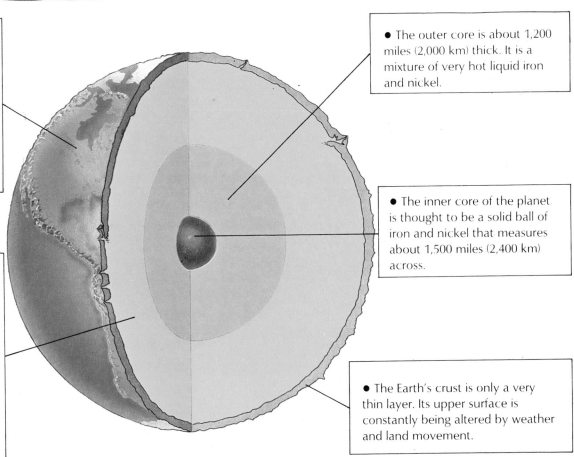

● The Earth's crust varies in thickness from 24.8 miles (40 km) beneath parts of the continents to only 3.1 miles (5 km) under parts of the ocean floor. It is made of lighter rock than the other layers. The temperature of the rocks increases by about 86°F (30°C) for every kilometer under the surface.

● The outer core is about 1,200 miles (2,000 km) thick. It is a mixture of very hot liquid iron and nickel.

● The inner core of the planet is thought to be a solid ball of iron and nickel that measures about 1,500 miles (2,400 km) across.

● The Earth's mantle is about 1,800 miles (2,900 km) thick. At the top it is made of solid rock. Deeper down it is so hot that the rock melts and becomes molten. The rock in the mantle layer is composed mainly of iron and magnesium.
　There is a definite boundary line between the crust and the mantle.

● The Earth's crust is only a very thin layer. Its upper surface is constantly being altered by weather and land movement.

## Riches from the Earth

Our main sources of **heat and power** come from beneath the Earth's surface. Oil, gas, and coal are called **fossil fuels**.

● Oil is made from the bodies of tiny sea creatures that lived millions of years ago. The bodies gathered on the seabed and they were gradually squeezed down under rocks that formed above them. Eventually they turned into oil.

● Coal is made from trees that died millions of years ago. Layers of the dead plant material were squeezed down until they turned into carbon.

● Natural gas is made when animal and plant bodies decompose. It is usually found in the same place as oil.

Ocean oil platform

## Gemstones

**Precious stones** are mined from beneath the Earth's surface.

● Gems form as crystals in igneous rock. They vary in color, shape, and size. Because they are rare, they have been prized for centuries.

● The rarest diamonds are blue or pink. Rubies are the rarest gems of all. The finest ones come from Myanmar (Burma).

● The best sapphires come from Myanmar (Burma), Kashmir, India, and Montana.

● The finest emeralds come from Colombia in South America.

# Volcanoes and Geysers

Toothpast◄

**V**olcanoes occur where hot liquid rock reaches the surface through cracks in the Earth's crust. Most volcanoes are found where two **plates** are pushing against one another or moving apart (see p8).

Volcanoes that erupt are called **active**. Many of them are found in an area around the Pacific Ocean called the "**Pacific Ring of Fire**."

Volcanoes in the Pacific Ring of Fire

Pacific Ocean

Volcanoes that might erupt are **dormant**. Volcanoes that have stopped erupting are **extinct**.

This volcano is active.

## How a volcano forms

**Pressure** builds up underground and pushes molten liquid rock up from a chamber beneath the surface. It spews out of a crack in the ground as **lava**.

Crater

Secondary cone

Layers of ash and lava.

- Ash, lava and rock build up to form a hill or mountain with a crater in the top. Sometimes, further eruptions of lava flow out of a secondary cone.

- Gas, lava, and pieces of solid rock (called tephra) spew out. Large molten lumps of tephra are called volcanic bombs.

Magma chamber

## Hot springs and geysers

**Hot springs** occur when underground water is heated up by hot rocks beneath the Earth's surface. The boiling water rises up through cracks in the ground.

**Geysers** are hot springs of water heated up under pressure. Many spout water and steam at regular intervals.

- Yellowstone Park in Wyoming has over 2,500 geysers, including a world-famous one nicknamed "Old Faithful."

- New Zealand and Iceland are the other main areas of geyser activity.

- A fumarole is a crack in the ground that releases more gas than water. These often occur on volcano slopes.

A fumarole

## Volcano shapes

A **volcano's shape** depends on the type of eruption that caused it and the sort of material that comes out.

- Shield volcanoes are shaped like upturned saucers, with gentle slopes.

- Cinder cone volcanoes are high, with steep slopes.

- Strata-volcanoes are cone-shaped mountains.

## Types of eruption

**Eruptions** are given different names, depending on how strong they are.

- Hawaiian eruptions are not very violent. They pour out liquid lava in fiery rivers.

- Strombolian eruptions pour out thicker lava, but not very violently. Strombolian volcanoes erupt continuously.

- Vulcanian eruptions produce violent explosions and throw out tephra, dust, gas, and ash.

- Peléean eruptions are gigantic explosions which throw out a huge cloud of gas and lava.

### Strange but true

- In 1783 an Icelandic eruption threw up enough dust to temporarily block out the Sun over Europe.

- The biggest known crater is on the planet Mars. It is 50 miles (80 km) wide and is three times higher than Mount Everest.

- Hot water from geysers is used to heat homes and offices in Reykjavic, capital of Iceland.

- About 20 to 30 volcanoes erupt each year, mostly under the sea.

## Volcanic islands

Many **ocean islands** have been formed by volcanic eruptions beneath the sea. First ash is blown above the water and then a pile of rock and lava builds up until it appears above the waves.

- In 1963 the volcanic island of Surtsey appeared near Iceland. It took three weeks to rise from the waves.

- In 1883 the volcanic island of Krakatoa, near Java, blew up. Rock blasted 50 miles (80 km) into the air.

## Pompeii

In A.D. 79 the Italian volcano **Vesuvius** erupted and buried the Roman cities of **Pompeii** and **Herculaneum**.

- The cities were hidden for nearly seventeen centuries, until a farmer discovered some ruins in 1748.

- Vesuvius is still an active volcano. If it erupted in the future, the nearby city of Naples would have to be evacuated.

# Earthquakes

Earthquakes are severe shocks that happen when powerful **vibrations** pass from underground up to the surface through solid rock. The ground shakes violently and huge cracks may appear. Some are wide enough to swallow cars.

Earthquakes happen where two of the Earth's **plates** meet. The pressure of the plates pushing against each other causes deep cracks in the rock called **fault lines**.

The rocks on either side of a fault line sometimes slide up or along. This makes them bend and shatter, causing earthquake **shock waves**.

Rock moves along the line.

Fault line

Focus of earthquake

## Earthquake profile

An earthquake begins beneath the ground at the point where the rocks move.

The movement creates **waves of energy** which travel up to the surface.

Epicenter on the surface

- The point where the earthquake begins underground is called the focus.

- The point on the surface above the focus is called the epicenter.

Shock waves

- There may be lots more minor earthquakes called aftershocks after the first earthquake. These occur because the rocks beneath are falling back into place.

Focus underground

## Earthquake areas

- Most earthquakes happen around the edges of the Pacific Ocean or near mountainous areas such as the Himalayas.

- The San Andreas Fault runs through California. In 1906, the rocks on one side of the fault moved 15 ft. (4.6 meters), causing an earthquake.

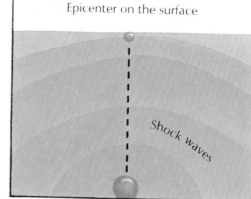

San Francisco

San Andreas Fault line

N

Los Angeles

## Earthquake buildings

- Earthquake-proof buildings are built with reinforced steel or concrete frames on a solid platform. Many skyscrapers in San Francisco are built this way.

## Earthquake effects

An earthquake can cause:

- A series of gigantic fast-moving waves called tsunami. The biggest one ever seen was 220 ft. (67 m) tall, the height of about 9 houses!

- Dangerous mud and rock avalanches that engulf the surrounding land.

- Fires set off by broken gas pipes and electrical cables.

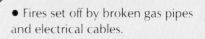

## Measuring earthquakes

Earthquakes are measured using the **Richter Scale** or the **Mercalli Scale**. The Richter Scale has 8 numbers that measure earthquake energy. Each number denotes 10 times more energy than the number before. The Mercalli Scale has 12 numbers measuring the effect of an earthquake on objects and buildings.

Examples of Richter numbers:

| 1·2 | 5 | 7 | 8 |
|---|---|---|---|
| Barely noticeable | Some damage | Like a nuclear bomb | Total devastation |

Examples of Mercalli numbers

| II | V | VII | XII |
|---|---|---|---|
| Lamps swing and windows shake | Dishes smash | Walls collapse | Total damage |

## Earthquake instruments

Seismograph

Instruments called seismographs are used to measure earthquakes.

● A seismograph uses a pen attached to a frame to draw a line on a drum. The line shows the force of the earthquake.

● The first seismograph was made in China in A.D. 150. It was a pot with dragon heads sticking out. Tremors made balls fall from the dragons' jaws into the mouths of frogs below. The side that the balls fell showed the direction of the quake epicenter.

Ball falling

## Predicting earthquakes

Scientists monitor earthquake areas to predict tremors. There are **monitoring stations** all over the world that measure Earth movement. Some early signs of earthquakes are shown below:

● A radioactive gas called radon is released from rocks. Scientists monitor well water to detect increases in radon traces.

● Small tremors called foreshocks happen just before an earthquake. The ground swells up and cracks.

● Animals behave oddly. They are often very sensitive to tremors.

### Strange but true

● The longest earthquake known lasted for 38 days.

● There are thousands of earthquakes a year. Only 20 to 30 are felt by people.

● In 1975 the Chinese city of Haicheng was evacuated 2 hours before an earthquake because people noticed their animals behaving oddly.

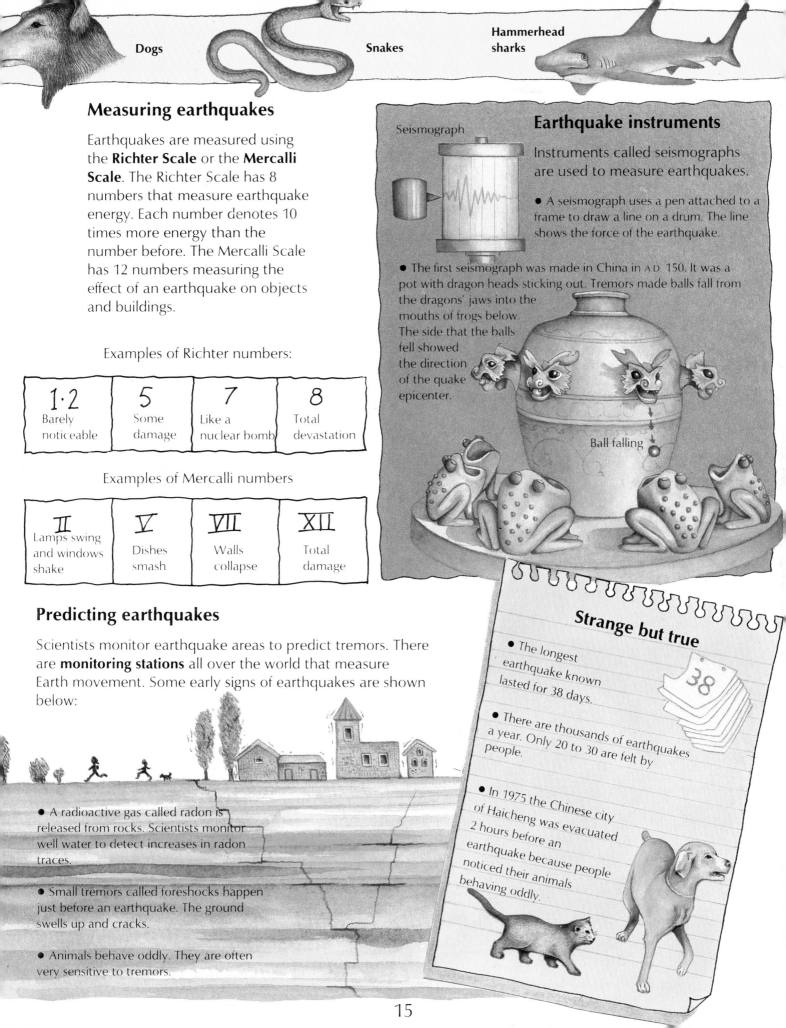

# Mountains and Valleys

Here are the highest land mountains in order of height:

Mt. Everest
Himalayas
29,028 ft.
(8,848 m)

Mountains are rock masses that are at least 2,000 ft. (600 m.) high. They are usually found in groups called **ranges** or **chains**. They cover about one quarter of the Earth's land surface.

A mountain range

Most of the world's tallest mountain ranges were built when two of the Earth's **plates** collided with each other, slowly pushing up the rock above. Mountain building takes millions of years. It is still going on today.

Fold mountains pushed up

## Types of mountain

There are four different types of mountain, called **fold**, **block**, **volcanic**, and **dome**.

Fold mountain

Block mountain

- Fold mountains occur when two of the Earth's plates push against each other. The rock in the middle is pushed up in folds.

- Sometimes two faults (deep rock cracks) run alongside each other. Pressure heaves up the block of land in the middle.

- A volcanic mountain grows when lava, dust and ashes gradually build up in a cone shape (see pp12–13).

- Dome mountains are created when hot volcanic material rises upward from deep in the Earth and pushes the rocks above into a dome shape.

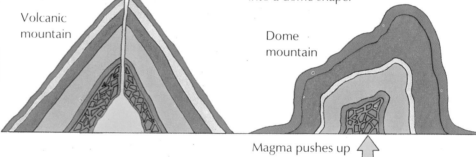

Volcanic mountain

Dome mountain

Magma pushes up

## Mountain areas

There are **mountain ranges** all over the world. The largest ones are shown on the map below.

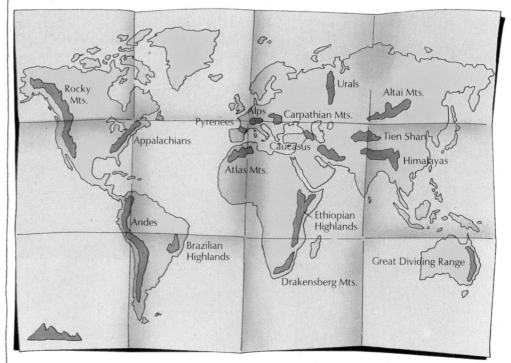

Rocky Mts.

Urals

Altai Mts.

Alps
Pyrenees

Carpathian Mts.

Appalachians

Caucasus

Tien Shan

Atlas Mts.

Himalayas

Andes

Ethiopian Highlands

Brazilian Highlands

Great Dividing Range

Drakensberg Mts.

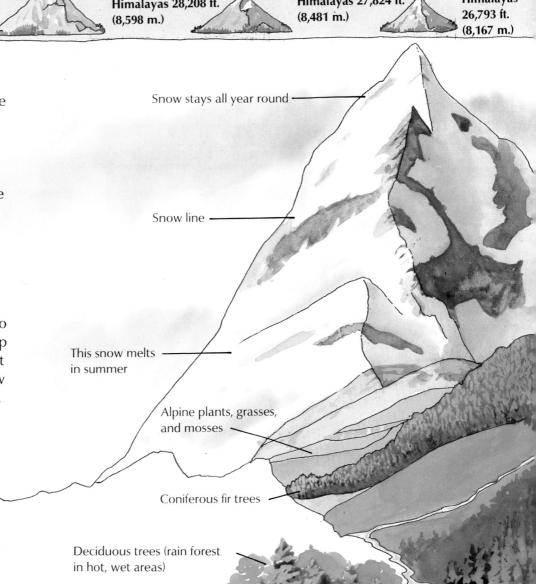

| K2 Himalayas 28,250 ft. (8,611 m) | Kanchenjunga Himalayas 28,208 ft. (8,598 m.) | Makalu Himalayas 27,824 ft. (8,481 m.) | Dhaulagiri Himalayas 26,793 ft. (8,167 m.) |

## Mountain profile

At the bottom of a mountain there may be a forest of **deciduous trees**, which lose their leaves in winter. In hot, wet areas, there may be **rain forest**.

Further up, there are likely to be **coniferous trees**. Most of these stay green all year round.

The place where the trees stop growing is called the **tree line**. Above this line only hardy alpine plants, grasses, and mosses grow.

Finally, the temperature gets too cold for plants to grow. On the top of high mountains it is so cold that there is snow all year round. Below this the snow will melt in summer. The line between the two areas is called the **snow line**.

Snow stays all year round

Snow line

This snow melts in summer

Alpine plants, grasses, and mosses

Coniferous fir trees

Deciduous trees (rain forest in hot, wet areas)

### Strange but true

● The Andes and the Himalayas are still rising, but their rocks are being worn away.

● The lowest officially-named hill stands 15 ft. (4.5 m.) high on a golf course in Brunei.

● Mount Everest is 20 times higher than the world's tallest building, the Sears Tower in Chicago.

## Glaciers and valleys

A **glacier** is a huge mass of ice that moves down a valley under its own weight. A glacier:

● Moves along very slowly.

● Carves out a U-shaped valley as it travels along.

When winter snow melts on a mountainside, the water flows into **rivers**. A river:

● Carves out a V-shaped valley as it travels.

● May carve a steep-sided valley called a gorge.

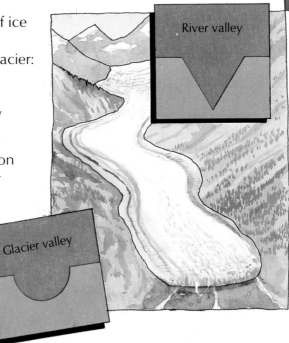

River valley

Glacier valley

# Rivers and Lakes

**R**ivers begin on higher land and flow downhill to the sea. They may start from **underground springs**, or from melting **snow** or **glaciers**.

A river's route is divided into three parts. The first part is called the **upper course**, where the river flows steeply downhill and the current is fast. The water carries sand, gravel, and rocks down with it.

Upper course

Middle course

Lower course

In the **middle course** the river flows along a gentler slope. It travels more slowly but it still wears away rock and sand from its banks.

In the **lower course** the river slows down and gets wider. Some of the sand and rock it has been carrying is now worn down into tiny particles called **silt**.

## River profile

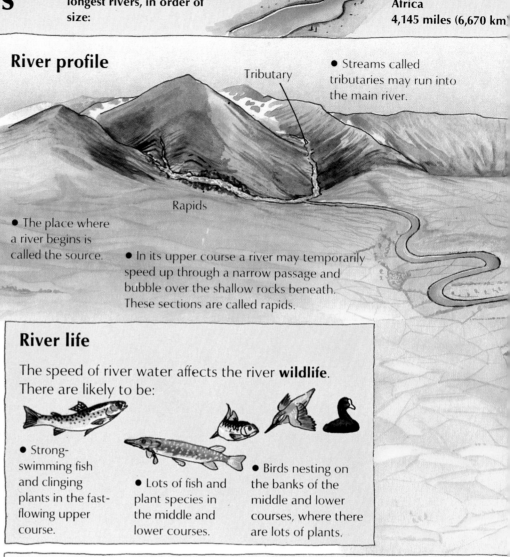

Tributary

- Streams called tributaries may run into the main river.

Rapids

- The place where a river begins is called the source.

- In its upper course a river may temporarily speed up through a narrow passage and bubble over the shallow rocks beneath. These sections are called rapids.

## River life

The speed of river water affects the river **wildlife**. There are likely to be:

- Strong-swimming fish and clinging plants in the fast-flowing upper course.

- Lots of fish and plant species in the middle and lower courses.

- Birds nesting on the banks of the middle and lower courses, where there are lots of plants.

## Lakes

A **lake** is an area of water surrounded by land. Lakes occur where water can collect in hollows in the ground, or behind natural or artificial barriers. Lakes can be:

- Very large. The world's biggest freshwater lake is Lake Superior in the U.S. and Canada. It covers a vast area of over 31,777 sq. miles (82,300 sq. km.)

- Very deep. The world's deepest lake is Lake Baykal in Russia. Its deepest crevice goes down 6,365 ft. (1,940 m).

**Amazon**
S. America 4,007 miles
(6,448 km)

**Yangtze**
Asia 3,915 miles
(6,300 km)

**Mississippi-Missouri**
N. America
3,741 miles (6,020 km)

● A river joins the sea at its mouth. Here there is an area where freshwater and seawater mix, called an estuary.

● In its middle course, the bends in a river become more obvious. They are called meanders.

● A small river that joins a larger one is called a tributary.

Meander

Oxbow lake

● Sometimes a river meander changes course, leaving behind a small lake called an oxbow lake.

Estuary

Mouth

## Deltas

When a river reaches its mouth, it is moving very slowly. Sometimes it is carrying lots of mud and silt which may be dropped in the river mouth to form islands. Such an area is called a **delta**.

● The Ganges and the Brahmaputra rivers meet in India and Bangladesh to form the world's largest delta. It is 300 miles (480 km) long and 100 miles (160 km) wide.

Delta

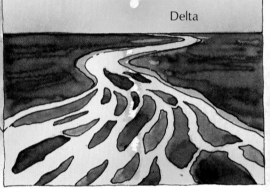

## Waterfalls

Most **waterfalls** occur where hard bands of rock cross the bed of a river. The river wears away the hard rock more slowly than softer rock downstream. Eventually this creates a steep drop.

● The world's highest waterfall is the Salto Angel Falls in Venezuela. It plunges down a cliff 3,212 ft. (979 m) high.

## Strange but true

● A huge underground river runs underneath the Nile, with six times more water than the river above.

● Lake Bosumtwi in Ghana formed in a hollow made by a meteorite.

● Beaver Lake, in Yellowstone Park was artificially created by beaver damming.

● The world's shortest river is the D River, Oregon. It is only 121 ft. (37 m.) long.

# Oceans

There are four large oceans on the Earth. They join together to form one huge mass of water. They are called the **Pacific**, the **Atlantic**, the **Indian**, and the **Arctic**.

Parts of the oceans are divided into smaller areas called **seas**. These are mostly around coastlines and islands.

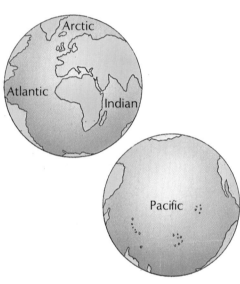

The **temperature** of seawater varies across the world. For instance, most of the water in the Arctic is permanently frozen, whereas in hot tropical areas the sea can reach the temperature of a warm bath.

## Ocean floor profile

If you were able to look beneath the ocean surface you would see:

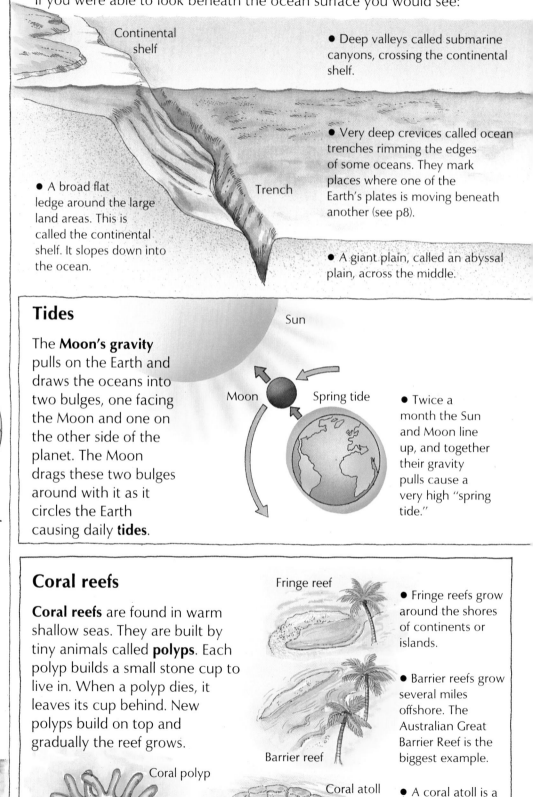

● Deep valleys called submarine canyons, crossing the continental shelf.

● Very deep crevices called ocean trenches rimming the edges of some oceans. They mark places where one of the Earth's plates is moving beneath another (see p8).

● A broad flat ledge around the large land areas. This is called the continental shelf. It slopes down into the ocean.

● A giant plain, called an abyssal plain, across the middle.

## Tides

The **Moon's gravity** pulls on the Earth and draws the oceans into two bulges, one facing the Moon and one on the other side of the planet. The Moon drags these two bulges around with it as it circles the Earth causing daily **tides**.

● Twice a month the Sun and Moon line up, and together their gravity pulls cause a very high "spring tide."

## Coral reefs

**Coral reefs** are found in warm shallow seas. They are built by tiny animals called **polyps**. Each polyp builds a small stone cup to live in. When a polyp dies, it leaves its cup behind. New polyps build on top and gradually the reef grows.

● Fringe reefs grow around the shores of continents or islands.

● Barrier reefs grow several miles offshore. The Australian Great Barrier Reef is the biggest example.

● A coral atoll is a broken ring of coral islands with water in the middle.

| Atlantic | Indian | Arctic |
|---|---|---|
| 31,660,000 sq. miles (82,000,000 sq. km) | 28,350,000 sq. miles (73,426,000 sq. km) | 4,700,000 sq. miles (12,173,000 sq. km) |

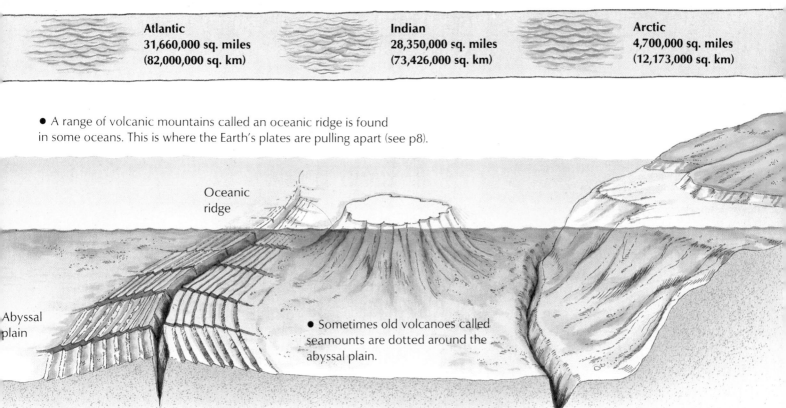

● A range of volcanic mountains called an oceanic ridge is found in some oceans. This is where the Earth's plates are pulling apart (see p8).

Oceanic ridge

Abyssal plain

● Sometimes old volcanoes called seamounts are dotted around the abyssal plain.

Sun

Neap tide

Moon

● When the Moon and Sun are at right angles the Sun opposes the Moon's gravity pull, causing a very low "neap tide."

## Currents

Water near the ocean surface travels around the world in **currents**. These movements are caused by winds, differences in water temperature and saltiness, coastline shape and the Earth's rotation.

● The world's largest current is the West Wind Drift, which flows between America and Antarctica.

## Strange but true

● Off the coast of Florida there is an underwater hotel. Guests have to dive to the entrance.

● There is one-seventh ounce (4 grams) of gold in every million tons of seawater.

● The biggest storm wave ever recorded was 111 ft. (34 m) high from crest to trough.

● Only about a ninth of an iceberg shows above the surface of the water.

## Sea riches

● Oysters, seaweed, and fish can be farmed in the sea. Some scientists have managed to build artificial reef "farms" and colonize them with lobsters and shellfish.

● Underwater communities could be built for marine farm workers. Some experiments have already been carried out using prototype underwater houses.

● On the deep ocean floor there are millions of rock lumps called manganese nodules. Manganese is used for hardening steel.

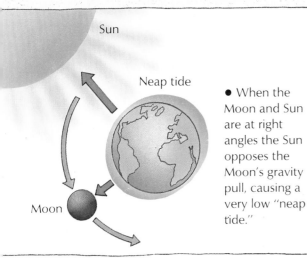

# Coastlines

A **coastline** is the place where the land meets the sea. Coastlines vary in shape and they have different features — for instance, one coastline might have gentle sloping **beaches**, whereas another might have rocky **cliffs** and **caves**.

## Coastal features

Coastlines do not always stay the same shape. As the sea pounds against a cliff coastline, it gradually wears down the rock to form features such as **caves** and **arches**.

● Seawater will get into cracks in the rock to hollow it out. If the rock is strong enough, the sea may hollow out a cave.

● Sometimes waves pound both sides of a headland and wear away an arch in the middle.

● Eventually arches collapse, leaving isolated rocks called stacks.

● Sometimes waves enlarge a cave so much that a crack appears in the roof. In rough weather water sprays out of the crack, called a blowhole.

## Beaches

The sea gathers loose rocks and stones as it wears away at the coastline. The waves grind them into tiny particles and then drop them onto the shore, forming **beaches**.

● The Hawaiian Islands have beaches made of black sand, formed by volcanic lava.

● The Bermuda Islands have pale pink beaches. The sand is made from fragments of red shell.

● The dazzling white beaches of Barbados are made of tiny shell fragments worn down by the sea.

● A stretch of beach on the Namibian coast in Africa provides the world's best supply of loose diamonds. They are hidden among the sand and gravel.

### Strange but true

● The mudskipper fish can climb up a mangrove tree and hang from a branch to wait for the tide to come in.

● The sea level is likely to rise over 12 inches (30 cm) over the next 100 years.

● Venice in Italy is built on 118 islets joined by 400 bridges. It is gradually sinking into the water.

**Guildfordia yoka,
Japan**

**Cittarium pica,
West Indies**

**Conus textile,
Indo-Pacific**

● Cliffs are sometimes made up of layers of different rock. You can often see the layers, called bedding planes, running along a cliff face.

## Marshes and estuaries

● Where a river meets the sea there may be an area of muddy plain called an estuary. The sea washes over the plain, creating mudflats, creeks, and salty marshes. Wading birds like to nest here.

● In hot tropical places, coastal marshes are often swamps filled with mangrove trees. These trees have a special root system that enables them to survive in salty water, and they can absorb oxygen from the air.

## Coastal life

Beaches provide a home for lots of different **animals** and **plants**. You might find:

● Seaweed, which is a plant without roots or a stem. It is made up of fronds and a rootlike "holdfast" at the bottom for anchoring the seaweed firmly onto rocks.

A limpet shell

● Limpets anchored firmly to the rocks. A limpet has a very powerful foot which works like a suction cup and clamps the shell firmly to the rock surface.

Worm casts

● Worm casts, which are small piled-up cones of wet sand. They are made by lugworms that burrow beneath the surface. The tiny worms swallow sand and digest the minute particles of food mixed up with it. Then they push out the waste, making casts on the sand surface.

● On some lowland coasts, sand blows up from the beach to form dunes. Marram grass is often planted to "fix" the dunes so that the sand does not blow away.

Marram grasses

● A bubble in the sand. Underneath, there may be a cockleshell. It burrows down and then it sticks two tiny siphons above the surface. One takes in seawater along with food particles. The other expels the waste water, creating the bubble that you can see.

A cockleshell

# The Sky

The Earth is surrounded by a layer of **gases** called the **atmosphere**. It is made up of five main layers. Each layer is at a different **temperature** and is made up of a mixture of different gases.

The boundaries between the different layers are not clear-cut.

## In the air

The atmosphere is made up of:

78.09 percent nitrogen

20.95 percent oxygen

0.93 percent argon

0.03 percent carbon dioxide, helium, hydrogen, methane, krypton, neon, ozone, xenon, and water vapor.

## Sky colors

**Sunlight** is made up of different **light waves**. The visible ones are red, orange, yellow, green, blue, indigo, and violet. These colors are called the **spectrum**. You can see them in a rainbow. The spectrum causes:

● Blue skies. When the Sun's rays reach the Earth's atmosphere, the blue light waves scatter in all directions. Provided the light is not obscured by cloud, it shows across the sky.

● The atmosphere is like a pale red filter, making all light from space slightly reddish. The Sun is very low in the sky at sunrise and sunset, and its rays shine through more air than at other times of day. This means that more sunlight is filtered by the atmosphere, causing red sunrises and sunsets.

## Air pressure

The layers of gases around the Earth press down on the surface. This force is called **air pressure**. It is strongest at ground level and gets weaker with height.

● High up on mountains the air pressure is weak and the air has less oxygen content than air down below.

● Aircraft cabins are artificially pressurized so that the passengers can breathe comfortably, even though they are flying high up in the atmosphere.

Low pressure

High pressure

## Strange but true

● Some early hot-air balloons were so heavy that the passengers stripped off to help keep the weight down.

● The Ancient Egyptians worshiped a sky goddess called Nut.

● The world's windiest place is Commonwealth Bay, Antarctica.

● In 1934 a gust of wind three times as strong as Beaufort scale 12 was measured on Mt. Washington, New Hampshire.

**Force 6 — strong breeze**
Large tree branches move

**Force 9 — strong gale**
Chimney pots crash
down

**Force 12 — hurricane**
Whole areas
devastated

## Atmosphere layers

The atmosphere is made up of these layers:

- The exosphere — height 300 to 5,000 miles (500 to 8,000 km) above the Earth's surface, merging into space.

Weather satellites orbit in the exosphere

- The thermosphere — height 50 to 300 miles (80 to 500 km). The temperature of this layer increases with height. At the top it is about 4,000°F (2,200°C).

When some spaceships re-entered orbit, their heat shields burned up in this layer, due to friction.

- The mesosphere — height 30 to 50 miles (50 to 80 km). The temperature of this layer gets colder with height. It varies from 50°F to −110°F (10°C to −80°C).

Unmanned balloons have measured the temperature in this layer

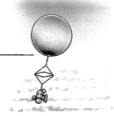

- The stratosphere — height 5 to 30 miles (8 to 50 km) (varies from place to place). This layer is cold, but the temperature increases with height. Within this layer is a band of ozone gas, which filters out the Sun's harmful rays.

Aircraft fly in this layer to avoid rough weather

- The troposphere — height up to 10 miles (16 km) over the equator, 5 miles (8 km) over the poles. This layer contains nearly all the water vapor and most of the other gases in the atmosphere. It gets colder with height.

Weather occurs in this layer

## The wind

The Sun's rays reflect upward off the ground, warming the air above it. **Warm air** is lighter and rises upward. **Cold air** is heavier and flows in to take the place of the air that has risen. This flowing air is **wind**.

- A current of rising warm air is called a thermal. Some birds like to find thermals. They spread out their wings and let the moving air carry them along. Gliders also use thermals to gain height.

- Some winds blow constantly in regular patterns around the world. Among the most constant are the Trade Winds which blow toward the equator from the Tropics.

- Anemometers are used to measure wind speed. The most common kind has three cups fixed onto a shaft. The stronger the wind, the faster the cups spin around. Their movement controls a dial that indicates speed.

# Weather

Here are some unusual weather facts and records:

Rainiest place: Kauai, Hawaii. Rain for 350 days a year

When water is warmed it **evaporates**, which means that it changes into an invisible gas called water **vapor**. When water vapor cools down it changes back into **liquid droplets**. When it gets very cold it becomes solid **ice crystals** that form snowflakes.

Six-sided snowflakes

## The water cycle

The **Sun** heats up the world's **oceans** and **lakes**. It makes water evaporate and rise upward. As the water vapor gets higher, it gets colder and changes into **water droplets**, which gather around specks of dust in the air. Billions of droplets together form a **cloud**. The droplets grow bigger until they are so heavy that they fall as **rain** back into the oceans and rivers.

Cloud

Ocean

## Strange but true

● Some people say they can smell rain. The smell may be gases produced by the damp soil.

● Italian farmers shoot fireworks into clouds to shatter hailstones that damage crops.

● Sea fog was once thought to be the breath of an underwater monster.

● At the South Pole the snow never melts.

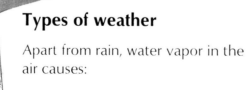

## Types of weather

Apart from rain, water vapor in the air causes:

● Snow, which occurs when it is very cold. Water droplets in the air freeze into ice crystals and fall to the ground.

● Fog, which can occur when the land or sea is cold and the air above it is warmer. The water vapor changes into a cloud of water droplets just above the surface.

● Hailstones, which begin as icy pellets in high storm clouds. They are buffeted about inside the cloud and gradually grow bigger as layers of ice freeze around them. Eventually they grow so heavy that they fall to the ground.

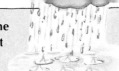

# Air masses

An **air mass** is formed when a vast area of air stays in the same place for some time. It gets warm or cold, depending on the temperature of the land or sea beneath.

When an air mass moves it brings weather changes.

Rain

● No new water is ever made in the atmosphere. Instead, the existing water recycles again and again.

● Rainbows, which appear on rainy days when the Sun is shining. You can only see one if you are standing with your back to the Sun. The sunlight shines on the raindrops in the air and is split up into the seven colors of the spectrum (see p.24).

● Dew, which occurs when air cools down at night and water vapor condenses into droplets of dew on the ground. The dew evaporates in the morning when the air warms up again.

# Clouds

There are ten different **kinds of cloud**. Each different shape gives a clue to the sort of weather you can expect.

● Cumulus clouds are fluffy, white puffs. They signal fine weather.

● Cirrus clouds are wisps with flicked-back tails. They may signal rain.

● Cirrostratus clouds thinly veil the Sun. They can bring rain or snow.

● Stratocumulus clouds spread out in uneven patches. They can mean dry weather.

● Cirrocumulus clouds look like ripples in the sky. They signal weather changes.

● Altostratus clouds make patchy thin layers. They may grow into rain clouds.

● Stratus clouds spread out in a low gray layer. They mean rain or snow.

● Cumulonimbus are billowing storm clouds that stretch high up into the sky.

● Nimbostratus clouds are dark low masses signaling rain or snow.

● Altocumulus clouds are fluffy cloud waves. They signal weather changes.

27

# Wild Weather

Sometimes the weather is dramatic and powerful. For instance, 45,000 **thunderstorms** take place every day and most of them are capable of producing as much energy as an atom bomb.

Violent **hurricanes** and **tornadoes** are regular weather features in some parts of the world.

## Thunderstorms

**Thunderstorms** occur when the air is warm and humid and rises upward very quickly, forming giant towering **cumulonimbus** storm clouds. Inside the clouds, ice crystals and water droplets whirl around, colliding with each other and creating tiny **electrical charges** as they do so. Gradually the charges build up until giant sparks flash from cloud to cloud or down to the ground and back.

- Lightning finds the quickest path to the Earth, so it usually hits high buildings or trees. Tall buildings are fitted with copper strips called lightning rods that carry the electric charge safely to the ground.

- You can tell how far away a storm is by counting the seconds between a lightning flash and a thunderclap. The storm is one mile away for every five seconds you count.

- Lightning travels down to the ground and then back up again along the same path. The journey is so fast that there only appears to be one flash.

- Lightning heats up the air in its path. The air expands rapidly, making the booming noise of thunder. Lightning and thunder occur at the same time, but you hear the thunder afterward because sound travels more slowly than light.

## Strange but true

- Cumulonimbus clouds can reach as high as 10 miles (15 km), nearly twice the height of Mount Everest!

- The ancient Chinese believed that storms were caused by dragons fighting in the sky.

- In 1940 a tornado uncovered buried gold and showered the coins over a Russian town.

- American Roy Sullivan has been struck by lightning a record seven times.

- Sheet lightning does not look like a long fork. Instead it looks like a momentary glow in the sky. It is caused by lightning flashing within a cloud.

 If you are in a car, stay inside it. You will be safe

 If you get stuck out in the open, crouch down or run for shelter

 Once you are indoors, you will be safe

# Tornadoes

**Tornadoes** are found mainly on the plains of North America, when small pockets of air rise quickly and create towering fast-spinning funnels of wind that leapfrog across the land. They can even lift up things in their path.

● There are about 640 tornadoes a year in North America, mostly in the plains states of Texas, Oklahoma, Kansas, and Nebraska. People who live in these areas have storm shelters in their homes to protect them if a tornado passes overhead.

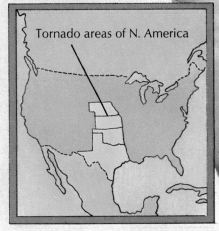

Tornado areas of N. America

● Tornado winds can spin at up to 400 mph (640 km/h). They have been known to lift heavy trains into the air.

● A waterspout is a tornado over the sea, a swirling air column that sucks up seawater. If a waterspout moves onto land, it drops its load. This has been known to cause surprise showers of fish and crabs!

# Hurricanes

**Hurricanes** are powerful tropical storms that occur in late summer and early autumn. They begin over warm seas near the equator, when warm air rises over a wide area and forms huge pillars of cloud full of water vapor.

Cold air rushes in beneath the warm air and a giant spinning wheel of whirling cloud begins to move over the sea surface.

● Hurricanes bring thousands of tons of rain and strong winds of up to 200 mph (320 km/h). They can do a great deal of damage if they reach a coastline.

● A hurricane may measure 250 miles (400 km) across. In the middle there is always a clear, calm patch called the eye. This may be about 25 miles (40 km) across.

● Hurricanes are given individual names. The first hurricane of the season is given a name beginning with A. The next one gets a name beginning with B, and so on.

● These storms are called hurricanes over the Atlantic Ocean, but in the Indian and Pacific oceans they are often called cyclones or typhoons.

● A tornado is quite different to a hurricane. It is much smaller, faster and more violent. Tornadoes are most frequent inland.

# Climate and Seasons

Here are some places that have unique climates:

Vostok, Antarctica. The coldest place on Earth; colder than a freezer

T he **climate** of a place is the pattern of weather it has from year to year.

Climate varies across the world. For instance, some places are always very cold or very warm, whereas in other areas the temperature changes from season to season.

**Seasons** vary from place to place. Some places have spring, summer, fall and winter. Other places may be hot all year, but have a wet and a dry season.

## Hot and Cold

The **Sun's rays** hit the Earth in straight lines, but because of the planet's round shape they spread out more at the poles than they do around the equator.

When the rays spread out they provide less heat, so the farther a place is from the equator, the colder its climate tends to be.

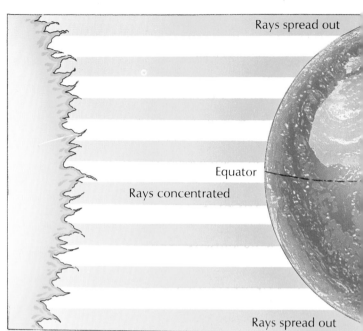

Rays spread out

Equator

Rays concentrated

Rays spread out

## Climate causes

**Ocean currents**, **distance from the sea**, **wind direction**, and **mountains** are all factors capable of having an effect on the climate of a particular place.

● Places near the sea have a "maritime" climate. They often have more rain, milder winters, and cooler summers than further inland. This is because the sea temperature does not vary as much as land temperature.

● Big cities often have a climate that is warmer than the surrounding land. Concrete buildings absorb the Sun's heat during the day and radiate it at night, warming the city air.

● Places that are far from the sea have a "continental" climate. The land heats up quickly but also cools down quickly, so there is a big temperature difference between summer and winter.

● The climate can vary within a very small area. For instance, in one garden there might be a cold shadowy corner alongside a warm sunny spot. Small areas like this are called microclimates.

 **Dallol, Ethiopia. The hottest place on Earth. Average temperature 94°F (34.4°C)**

 **Sahara Desert. The sunniest place on Earth**

**Verkhoyansk, NE Siberia. Biggest temp. range. From −94°F (−70°C) to 98°F (36.7°C)**

# World climates

The world is divided into six main **types of climate**. They are:

- Polar — cold all year, with a small amount of snowfall.

- Temperate — summers are warm at the coast and hot inland. Winters are cool at the coast and can be very cold inland.

- Equatorial — hot and wet all year round.

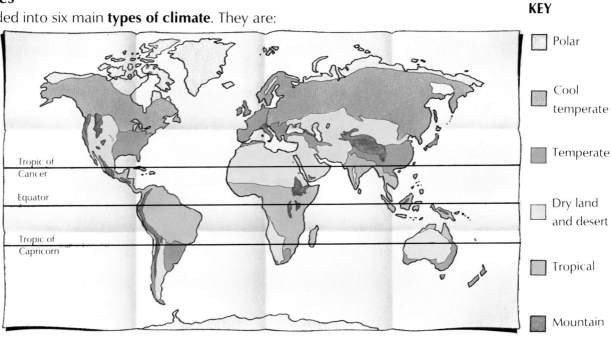

**KEY**

- Polar
- Cool temperate
- Temperate
- Dry land and desert
- Tropical
- Mountain

Tropic of Cancer

Equator

Tropic of Capricorn

# Seasons

The **seasons** are caused by the **Earth's orbit**. For a few months each year half the Earth is tilted toward the Sun and gets strong heat rays, while the other half is tilted away and gets weak rays.

The position is gradually reversed through the year. When it is **summer** in one hemisphere it is **winter** in the other.

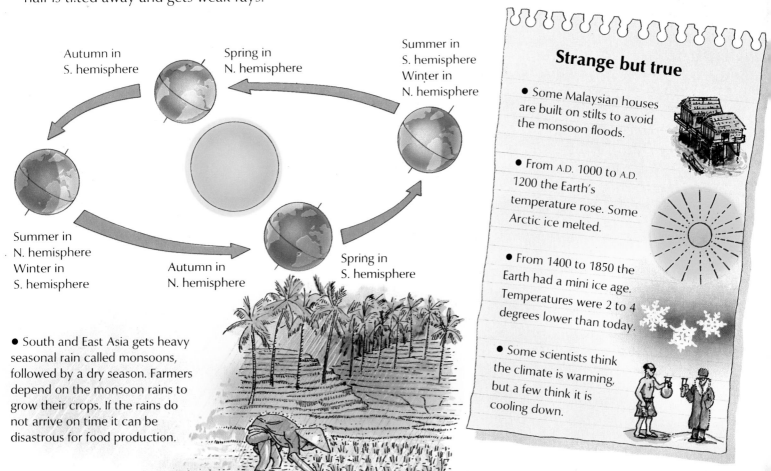

Autumn in S. hemisphere

Spring in N. hemisphere

Summer in S. hemisphere
Winter in N. hemisphere

Summer in N. hemisphere
Winter in S. hemisphere

Autumn in N. hemisphere

Spring in S. hemisphere

- South and East Asia gets heavy seasonal rain called monsoons, followed by a dry season. Farmers depend on the monsoon rains to grow their crops. If the rains do not arrive on time it can be disastrous for food production.

## Strange but true

- Some Malaysian houses are built on stilts to avoid the monsoon floods.

- From A.D. 1000 to A.D. 1200 the Earth's temperature rose. Some Arctic ice melted.

- From 1400 to 1850 the Earth had a mini ice age. Temperatures were 2 to 4 degrees lower than today.

- Some scientists think the climate is warming, but a few think it is cooling down.

# Plant Life

There are more than 335,000 known **plant species**. They are vital to life on Earth because they produce the oxygen that animals need in order to survive.

Plants grow in most parts of the world. The type of **vegetation** that grows in a particular place depends on the **climate** and the type of **soil** there is to be found in the area.

## Food-making

Many plants make their own **food**. In the process they create oxygen and use up **carbon dioxide**.

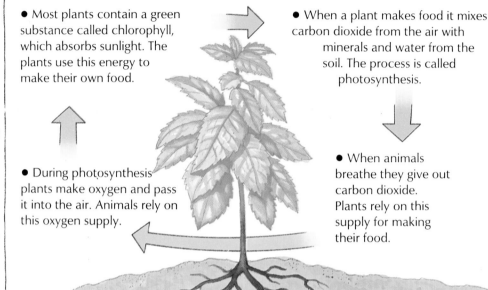

● Most plants contain a green substance called chlorophyll, which absorbs sunlight. The plants use this energy to make their own food.

● When a plant makes food it mixes carbon dioxide from the air with minerals and water from the soil. The process is called photosynthesis.

● During photosynthesis plants make oxygen and pass it into the air. Animals rely on this oxygen supply.

● When animals breathe they give out carbon dioxide. Plants rely on this supply for making their food.

## Flowering plants

Many plants grow from **seeds**, and in order for a new plant seed to grow, a tiny **pollen grain** containing a male cell must join with a female cell inside an **ovule**. Some plants produce **flowers** and these contain pollen and ovules.

● Some flowers contain sweet nectar which insects feed on. When an insect visits a flower, tiny pollen grains brush onto its coat. It carries them to the next flower it visits and they join together with the ovules in the new flower.

● Some flowering plants, such as grasses, do not attract insects. Instead, they rely on the wind to blow their pollen to other plants.

● After plants are pollinated, some begin to grow seeds. The seeds eventually drop to the ground. If the weather and the soil conditions are right, they grow into new plants.

## Strange but true

● The baobab tree can hold up to 260 gallons (1000 liters) of water in its trunk.

● The oldest living tree is a Californian bristlecone pine named "Methuselah." It is about 4,700 years old.

● Bamboo can grow up to 3 feet (90 cm) a day.

● There were no grasses in the age of the dinosaurs — only ferns, conifers, and cycad plants.

 **Rubber trees — the white latex is collected to make rubber**

 **Conifers — softwood trunks are used to make woodpulp for paper**

**Cotton plants — the fluffy parts are used to make cotton**

# Plants around the world

Botanists divide the Earth into six different regions called **biomes**. Each biome is characterized by particular types of plants that grow there. The main biomes are shown below.

● Tropical rain forests cover about 6 percent of the Earth. They grow in a belt around the equator. Because there is so much rain in these areas there is a rich variety of plants, more than in any other region in the world.

● North of the deserts there are temperate forests of bushy-shaped broad-leaved trees. These are deciduous, which means they shed their leaves in autumn and grow new ones in spring.

● North of the temperate forests there is a huge belt of coniferous forest which covers a quarter of the Earth. Coniferous trees can survive the cold well. They have tough waxy-coated evergreen needles instead of broad leaves.

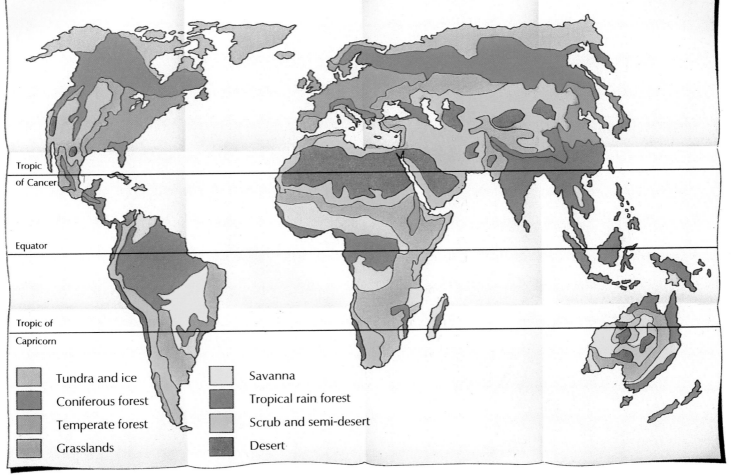

Tropic of Cancer

Equator

Tropic of Capricorn

| | | | |
|---|---|---|---|
| ▨ Tundra and ice | | ▨ Savanna | |
| ▨ Coniferous forest | | ▨ Tropical rain forest | |
| ▨ Temperate forest | | ▨ Scrub and semi-desert | |
| ▨ Grasslands | | ▨ Desert | |

● North of the coniferous forests lies the tundra, an area where the ground is permanently frozen a few inches beneath the surface. Therefore large trees cannot grow here. Instead there are carpets of moss and tiny flowers.

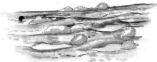

● Grasslands are areas where it is too dry for forests to grow but there is enough rain to stop the land being a desert. Carpets of tough grass grow here, weathering warm summers and cold winters. Grasslands near the equator are called savanna.

● A fifth of the Earth's surface is desert, where there is little or no rainfall. Plants which grow here must be able to survive in drought conditions. Many of them have leathery leaves and thick, rubbery flesh for storing moisture.

33

# Rain Forests

**R**ain forests are dense forests that grow in areas of **heavy rainfall** around the **equator**. They are found in West Africa, Southeast Asia, South America and the islands of the western Pacific.

Rain forests of the world

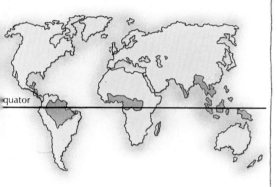

quator

Rain forests provide a home for the widest variety of animals and plants to be found anywhere in the world. For instance, in just one small area of the **Amazon** rain forest in South America there are likely to be hundreds of different kinds of trees and animals.

## Rain forest layers

Different types of **animals** and **plants** are found living at different heights in rain forest trees.

- Extra-tall trees called emergents grow above the rest of the jungle at heights between 145 and 200 ft. (45 and 60 m). Giant eagles nest in them.

- Lots of animals live in the canopy. This layer grows from about 100 to 150 ft. (30 to 45 m) high. It is rich in flowers and fruit.

- Ropelike plants called lianas grow up the tree trunks. Animals hang on to them to swing between branches.

200 ft.

130 ft.

65 ft.

15 ft.

- Small saplings and shrubs form the understory layer, rising to about 30 ft. (10 m) high.

- On the ground there is a thin layer of rotting leaves and vegetation called "leaf litter." It provides a home for many insects and fungi.

- The trees spread their roots out near the surface to gather all the food and moisture they can. Some of them grow big flat buttress roots to support their weight.

## Rain forest plants

- Rain forest trees flower at different times. Many of them have bright petals and sweet nectar to attract birds and insects to pollinate them (see p.32).

- In some rain forests hummingbirds feed on the nectar from flowers. They hover in front of a flower, beating their wings so fast that they make a humming noise. They dip their beaks into each bloom and suck out the nectar with their tongues.

- Many different plants festoon themselves around the forest trees, dangling their roots in the air to pick up moisture.

# Rain forest animals

**Mammals**, **birds**, **fish**, **insects**, **amphibians**, and **reptiles** can all be found in the South American rain forests.

Jaguar

● Rain forest mammals include tree-living cats such as jaguars and margays.

● Jungle reptiles include lizards and snakes of all kinds and sizes.

Anaconda

● Jungle insects include ants, butterflies, termites, and beetles of all different kinds.

● Some jungle leaves collect pools of water that attract many kinds of tree frog. Most tree frogs have suckers on their hands and feet to anchor them securely to branches.

Tree frog

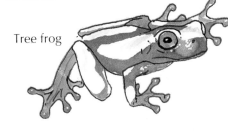

● Bright macaws, parrots, and toucans are just a few of the birds that nest in the jungle canopy.

Macaw

● Monkeys of all kinds swing from the jungle trees. Most South American monkeys have prehensile tails which they can use as an extra hand to grab onto things.

● Rain forests have rivers teeming with fish. The Amazon river is home to the ferocious piranha.

Piranha

## Strange but true

● The goliath beetle is found in African jungles. It grows up to 6 inches (14 cm) long and when it flies it sounds like a small aircraft.

● Amazon army ants sometimes travel in groups up to 20 million strong. They destroy and eat everything in their path.

● Gibbon monkeys look acrobatic, but in fact many of them suffer from broken limbs through falling.

# Rain forest people

The **people** who live in rain forests are usually grouped in small **tribes**.

● Some rain forest people survive by hunting for meat and gathering plants. They have a great knowledge of the rain forests and know exactly where to find food supplies.

● The traditional livelihoods of the rain forest Indians are increasingly threatened by forest clearing and mining projects. International efforts are being made to help them.

# Deserts

Deserts are places where less than 10 inches (25 cm) of rain falls per year. Food and water are scarce in these inhospitable regions.

There are lots of different types of **desert landscape**, ranging from sand dunes to rocky plains and mountains. Desert edges have more rain and are sometimes called semi-desert.

Deserts occur for several reasons. Some deserts are so far from the sea that by the time wind reaches them, all the moisture in the air has gone.

Some deserts are dry because they are near mountains. All the moisture in the air falls as rain and snow on the mountain tops before it reaches the desert on the other side.

## Deserts of the world

The world's main **desert areas** are shown below:

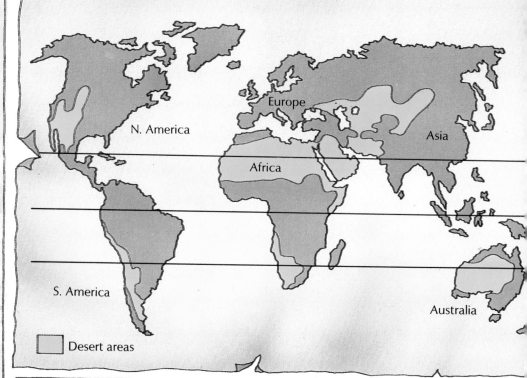

Europe

N. America

Asia

Africa

S. America

Australia

☐ Desert areas

## Desert plants

**Desert plants** are adapted to drought:

● They gather water through their roots, which either spread out near the surface to soak up dew or grow deep down to moist soil layers.

● Some cacti have pleated skins that stretch so they can store water.

● The biggest cactus is the saguaro, found in the Sonoran Desert in southwest U.S.A. It can grow to 50 ft. (15 m) high.

● Many desert plants only flower and seed themselves when rains come. The plant seeds then lie in the ground for years until the next rain shower comes along.

Desert flower

Saguaro cactus

● Desert plants often have bright beautiful flowers that only appear for a short time after rain has fallen. They don't live long, so they must attract pollinating insects quickly. That is why their petals are so colorful.

• North American deserts have rocky plains, deep ravines, salt lakes, and canyons. The hottest place is Death Valley, California, where temperatures can reach over 130°F (56°C).

• The North African Sahara is the world's biggest desert, covering an area almost the size of the U.S. Most of it is rocky. Only about a tenth of it is covered in sand dunes.

• A belt of desert stretches down the west coast of South America. It includes the Atacama Desert in Chile, the driest place in the world. Droughts there last for hundreds of years.

• Much of central Australia is a semi-desert called the Outback. It is dotted with rocky outcrops such as the famous Ayers Rock.

Ayers Rock

• The Arabian Desert is partly a sea of sand with dunes up to 800 ft. (240 m) high. Bedouin tribes travel the desert, camping in tents wherever they stop.

• The Gobi Desert in central Asia has hot summers and severe winters. The people who live there are nomads. They spend their lives traveling the barren, rocky land in search of grazing for their yak herds.

Yak and tribesman

• The Kalahari Desert in southern Africa is on a huge plateau. In the middle there is a sea of red sand dunes. The Kalahari bushmen hunt and gather food from this wilderness.

Kalahari bushman

## Desert animals

**Desert animals** usually shelter during the heat of the day and come out when the temperature drops in the evening. They get the moisture they need from eating plants or other creatures.

• Most desert spiders do not build webs. Instead they hunt for food. The camel spider is one of the largest desert specimens. It spans up to 6 inches (15 cm).

• Camels can survive for many days without water. Their nostrils can close up to keep out the dust.

• Desert reptiles include all kinds of snakes and lizards. They stay in the shade when they can.

### Strange but true

• Prehistoric paintings show the Sahara as fertile land.

• Early European explorers of the Australian Outback took a boat with them. They were looking for a fabled lake.

• In Saudi Arabia there are solar-powered pay phones in the desert.

• Ostriches sometimes eat sand, probably to help their digestion.

# Polar Regions

The **Arctic** and the **Antarctic** are the coldest regions in the world.

The Arctic is the area inside the **Arctic Circle**, which is a line of latitude below the North Pole. The **Arctic Ocean** is in the middle, and is frozen in winter. The land around the edge is **tundra** (see p33).

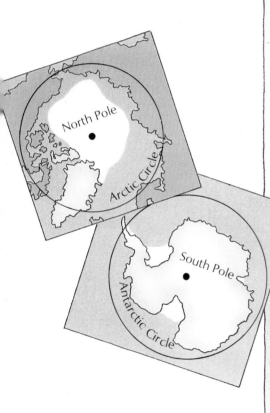

The **Antarctic** is a continent surrounding the South Pole. It covers over 9 percent of the Earth's surface.

Most of the Antarctic land is covered by a thick sheet of ice. Wildlife is found only around the coasts and on outlying islands, where the temperature is warmer than it is inland.

## The Arctic

For most of the year the Arctic **tundra** is covered in snow. In the brief summer months the snow melts, but cannot drain away because under the land surface there is a permanently frozen layer of earth called **permafrost**. Instead the water gathers in lakes, pools and bogs.

- Sometimes the wind whips up the Arctic snow and causes "white outs" which are rather like sandstorms in the desert. White outs can start suddenly and last for days.

- Most Arctic animals are to be found on the tundra. They arrive in summer and migrate south or hibernate underground in winter.

- Tundra plants are small. They grow near the ground to avoid the biting winds and cold temperatures. Some of them have hairy stems that help to keep them warm.

## The Antarctic

The Antarctic is the **coldest** and **windiest** place on Earth. Its ice sheets hold a large amount of the Earth's permanent ice. In the Antarctic:

- The tops of high mountains only just peek above the ice, which is up to $2\frac{1}{2}$ miles (4 km) thick in parts.

- The world's biggest icebergs, up to 60 miles (100 km) wide, break off from the coastal ice shelf and drift far out to sea. This process of breaking off is called "calving."

- Some areas of coastal land are exposed in summer. Algae and lichen grow here, but there are hardly any other plants.

Killer whale

Minke whale

Humpback whale

- Many Arctic animals have white fur, which camouflages them against snow. For instance, the Arctic hare is very hard to spot against a wintery background.

Arctic hare

- The coat of the Arctic caribou is ideal for keeping warm. Each hair is hollow so that it can trap warm air inside.

Caribou

- Some Arctic animals are plant eaters and some are hunters. The polar bear is the fiercest of them all. Its main prey is the ringed seal.

Polar bear

- The Arctic is already being used for natural resources such as oil. Its development must be planned very carefully, so as not to damage the lives of its unique animals.

## Strange but true

- The biggest animal found on inland Antarctica is the housefly.

- The Antarctic notothenia fish has a protein in its blood that acts like antifreeze and stops the fish freezing in icy sea.

- Penguins are so well insulated by fat that they often overheat when they are active. They have to stand with their beaks open to cool down.

- The Adelie penguin can leap four times its own height to get from sea to land.

## Life in the Antarctic

- Tiny mites are found in parts of the Antarctic where no other creatures could survive. The mites can live at temperatures below $-75°F$ $(-60°C)$.

Mite

- Nearly all the birds that visit the Antarctic coast are seabirds.

Albatross

Petrel

Skua

- Twelve species of whale visit the area, including the mighty blue whale, the biggest animal on Earth.

Blue whale

Emperor penguin

- Six species of seal live around the coast. They spend most of their time in the water but they go on land to breed.

- Many Antarctic animals feed on tiny floating animals and plants called plankton. Plankton animals, called zooplankton, gather in shoals off the coast.

- The Antarctic may be rich in oil and minerals deep beneath the surface. Conservationists are trying to limit drilling and mining because of the damage it would do to the environment.

Elephant seal

# Saving the Earth

The Earth's rivers, seas, and soil are threatened by **pollution**. It even affects the air we breathe. Scientists have realized that pollution is getting worse and that the whole planet will be seriously harmed unless something is done quickly to limit the damage.

## Air pollution alert

**Carbon dioxide** ($CO_2$) in the atmosphere traps some of the Sun's heat. The level of carbon dioxide, and some other gases, has been rising so much through pollution that the Earth's **climate** may warm up as a result. Air pollution is increased by:

- Fumes from car exhausts, factories and power stations.

- Burning or cutting down forests. The burning releases fumes and the destruction of plants means that less $CO_2$ is taken out of the atmosphere.

- CFCs, which are chemicals used in some aerosols, refrigerators, and air-conditioning systems. They destroy the ozone layer which protects us from harmful ultraviolet rays (see p.25).

## Forest alert

It is estimated that **1 sq. mile of rain forest** is destroyed every 6 minutes. If this continues, the rain forests will disappear by the year 2050. The destruction of the rain forests is caused by:

- People clearing vast areas to graze their cattle herds.

- Flooding caused by hydroelectric dams being built across rivers.

- Chopping down hardwood trees to make products such as mahogany furniture.

## Strange but true

- The U.S. uses 29 percent of the world's gasoline and 33 percent of the world's electricity.

- Some Chinese farmers use flocks of ducks to kill harmful insects.

- The industrial complex of Cubatao in Brazil is known as the Valley of Death because its pollution has destroyed the trees and rivers nearby.

## Water alert

The world's **rivers** and **oceans** are gradually becoming more polluted. The pollution is caused by:

- Factories discharging polluted waste straight into rivers and seas.

- Oil leaking into the sea from ships and oil terminals.

- Artificial fertilizer and pesticide chemicals washed into the water supply by rainfall.

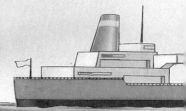

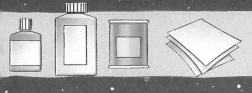

## Air pollution action

People are trying to reduce global warming by:

- Fitting industrial chimneys with filters that clean up waste fumes.

- Fitting catalytic converters to cars to clean up exhaust fumes.

- Recycling as many products as possible, such as glass, aluminum cans, and paper.

- Developing new fuels to replace gasoline.

- Phasing out the use of CFCs.

- Trying to stop the destruction of the world's forests.

## Forest action

People are trying to save the rain forest by:

- Passing laws to limit the destruction of these forests.

- Offering financial help to countries where there are rain forests, to persuade them to stop cutting down the trees.

- Refusing to buy rain forests hardwood products such as mahogany.

## Water action

People are trying to cut down water pollution by:

- Making it illegal for factories to dump untreated waste and for farmers to use dangerous chemicals.

- Finding more effective ways of getting rid of oil slicks.

# Earth Facts and Lists

## The Earth in Space

● The distance between the Earth and the Moon is 238,884 miles (384,365 km).

● Light from the Sun takes about 8 minutes to reach the Earth.

● The Earth's nearest star, apart from the Sun, is Proxima Centauri.

● Light from Proxima Centauri takes more than four years to reach Earth.

● The average speed of the Earth in orbit is 18.5 miles (29.8 km) per second.

● The Earth's density is 5.517 times the density of water.

● The Earth tilts on its axis at an angle of 23.5°.

● The light we see from the Moon at night does not really come from the Moon itself. What we see is light from the Sun shining onto the Moon's surface.

## The Earth from birth

● If history up to A.D. 1 was squashed into a scale of one year, with the Earth's birth on 1 January, the first life on Earth wouldn't begin until the end of March.

● The first dinosaurs would appear in the middle of December.

● The first people would emerge only a few hours before the end of the year.

## The Earth's surface

● The Earth's total surface area is 196,950,000 sq. miles (510,100,000 sq. km).

● The total land area of the Earth is 57,400,000 sq. miles (148,800,000 sq. km).

● It would take you about 6 months to jog around the Earth without stopping.

## Largest countries

The ten largest countries:

| Country | Size |
| --- | --- |
| Russia | 6,592,800 sq. miles |
| Canada | 3,851,790 sq. miles |
| China | 3,695,483 sq. miles |
| U.S.A. | 3,618,770 sq. miles |
| Brazil | 3,286,473 sq. miles |
| Australia | 2,967,895 sq. miles |
| India | 1,269,340 sq. miles |
| Argentina | 1,072,158 sq. miles |
| Kazakhstan | 1,049,150 sq. miles |
| Sudan | 967,495 sq. miles |

## Islands

The world's largest islands and their areas:

| Island | Area |
| --- | --- |
| Greenland | 840,000 sq. miles |
| New Guinea | 317,000 sq. miles |
| Borneo | 287,400 sq. miles |
| Madagascar | 226,657 sq. miles |
| Baffin Island | 183,810 sq. miles |
| Sumatra | 182,859 sq. miles |
| Honshu | 88,976 sq. miles |
| Great Britain | 84,186 sq. miles |
| Ellesmere Island | 82,118 sq. miles |
| Victoria Island | 81,929 sq. miles |

## Peninsulas

A peninsula is a piece of land with water on three sides. These are the world's largest:

| Peninsula | Area |
| --- | --- |
| Arabia | 1,254,000 sq. miles |
| Southern India | 800,000 sq. miles |
| Alaska | 580,000 sq. miles |
| Labrador | 502,000 sq. miles |
| Scandinavia | 309,000 sq. miles |
| Iberian Peninsula | 225,000 sq. miles |

## Volcanoes

Here are the ten highest volcanoes that have been active this century:

| Volcano | Height | Country |
| --- | --- | --- |
| Ojos del Salado | 22,606 ft. | Argentina/Chile |
| San Pedro | 20,325 ft. | Chile |
| Guallatiri | 19,869 ft. | Chile |
| San José | 19,406 ft. | Chile |
| Cotopaxi | 19,334 ft. | Ecuador |
| Ubinas | 18,721 ft. | Peru |
| Lascar | 18,495 ft. | Chile |
| Tupungato | 18,492 ft. | Chile |
| Islaguga | 18,577 ft. | Chile |
| Popocatepetl | 17,872 ft. | Mexico |

● Toba in north-central Sumatra has the largest volcanic crater, with an area of 685 sq. miles (1,775 sq. km).

● When Laki in Iceland erupted in 1783, its lava flow stretched 40 miles (65 km), the longest ever recorded.

● There are over 750 active volcanoes in the world.

● About 10 percent of all volcanoes are underwater.

● Lava from an erupting volcano may be as hot as 2,200°F (1,200°C).

● When Mount Tolbachik in Russia erupted, lava poured out at more than 330 ft. (100 m) per second.

● One eruption from Mauna Loa (in Hawaii) lasted 1½ years.

● The loudest noise ever known was produced by a volcanic eruption at Krakatoa, near Java, in 1883. The sound was heard in Australia, 3,000 miles (5,000 km) away.

● The highest volcano, Cerro Aconcagua 22,830 ft. (6,960 m), is in the Andes. It is now extinct.

● Lava can take years to cool down.

## Mountains

● About 25 percent of all land is more than 30,000 ft. (900 m) above sea level.

● The further up a mountain you go, the colder the air becomes. The temperature drops by 35.6°F (2°C) for every 1,000 ft. (300 m) you climb.

● Tibet is the highest country in the world. Its average height above sea level is 14,760 ft. (4,500 m).

● Some of the oldest mountains in the world are the Highlands in Scotland. They are estimated to be about 400 million years old.

## Highest mountains

Here are the seven continents and their highest mountains:

| Continent | Mountain | Height |
|---|---|---|
| Africa | Kilimanjaro | 19,328 ft. |
| Antarctica | Vinson Massif | 16,852 ft. |
| Asia | Everest | 29,010 ft. |
| Australia | Cook | 12,305 ft. |
| North America | McKinley | 20,308 ft. |
| South America | Aconcagua | 22,820 ft. |
| Europe | Elbrus | 18,469 ft. |

## Longest ranges

Here are some of the longest mountain ranges:

| Mountain range | Length | Location |
|---|---|---|
| Andes | 4,500 mi. | South America |
| Rockies | 3,748 mi. | North America |
| Himalayas | 2,400 mi. | Asia |
| Great Dividing Range | 2,250 mi. | Australia |
| Trans-Antarctic | 2,200 mi. | Antarctica |

## Rivers

Here are the eleven longest rivers:

| River | Length | Location |
|---|---|---|
| Nile | 4,145 mi. | Africa |
| Amazon | 4,007 mi. | South America |
| Yangtze | 3,915 mi. | Asia |
| Mississippi/ Missouri | 3,741 mi. | North America |
| Yenisey/ Angara | 3,443 mi. | Asia |
| Huang Ho | 3,396 mi. | Asia |
| Ob/Irtysh | 3,362 mi. | Asia |
| Zaire | 2,921 mi. | Africa |
| Lena/Kirenga | 2,735 mi. | Asia |
| Amur | 2,700 mi. | Asia |
| Mekong | 2,600 mi. | Asia |

## Rivers and Lakes

● The highest lakes are in the Himalayan mountains, but the highest navigable lake is Lake Titicaca in the Andes, which is 12,500 ft. (3,811 m) above sea level.

● The deepest lake is Lake Baikal in Russia. At its deepest point it is almost $1\frac{1}{4}$ miles (2 km) deep.

● Fresh water from the Amazon River can be found up to 112 miles (180 km) out to sea.

● The muddiest river is the Huang Ho, or Yellow River, in China.

● The largest swamp is in the basin of the Pripyat River in Ukraine and Belarus. It covers an area of 29,174 sq. miles (46,950 sq. km).

## Lakes

Some of the largest lakes in the world:

| Lake | Area | Location |
|---|---|---|
| Caspian Sea | 143,552 sq. miles | Russia/Iran/ Azerbaijan/ Kazakhstan/ Turkmenistan |
| Superior | 31,795 sq. miles | Canada/ U.S.A. |
| Victoria | 26,834 sq. miles | Africa |
| Huron | 23,011 sq. miles | Canada/ U.S.A. |
| Michigan | 22,394 sq. miles | U.S.A. |
| Aral Sea | 15,444 sq. miles | Kazakhstan/ Uzbekistan |
| Tanganyika | 12,703 sq. miles | Africa |
| Great Bear | 12,278 sq. miles | Canada |
| Baikal | 11,776 sq. miles | Russia |

## Glaciers

These are the longest glaciers:

| Glacier | Length | Country |
|---|---|---|
| Lambert Fischer Ice Passage | 320 mi. | Antarctica |
| Novaya Zemlya | 260 mi. | Russia |
| Arctic Institute Ice Passage | 225 mi. | Antarctica |
| Nimrod/Lennox/ King Ice Passage | 180 mi. | Antarctica |
| Denman Glacier | 150 mi. | Antarctica |
| Beardmore Glacier | 140 mi. | Antarctica |
| Recovery Glacier | 140 mi. | Antarctica |
| Petermanns Gletscher | 124 mi. | Greenland |

## Earthquakes

The strongest earthquakes recorded are:

| Date | Country | Strength on Richter Scale |
|---|---|---|
| 1906 | Ecuador | 8.6 |
| 1929 | China | 8.6 |
| 1950 | India | 8.6 |
| 1952 | Russia | 8.5 |
| 1964 | Alaska | 8.4 |

Some of the most disastrous earthquakes:

| Date | Country | Number of people killed |
|---|---|---|
| 1556 | China | 830,000 |
| 1908 | Italy | 80,000 |
| 1920 | China | 180,000 |
| 1923 | Japan | 142,807 |
| 1976 | China | 655,237 |
| 1990 | Iran | 36,000 |

# Earth Facts and Lists

## Waterfalls

These are some of the largest waterfalls and the countries they are in:

| Waterfall | Total height | Country |
|---|---|---|
| Angel | 3,210 ft. | Venezuela |
| Tugela | 8,606 ft. | South Africa |
| Utigard | 2,623 ft. | Norway |
| Mongefossen | 2,538 ft. | Norway |
| Yosemite | 2,423 ft. | U.S.A. |
| Ostre Mardola Foss | 2,151 ft. | Norway |
| Tyssestrengane | 2,118 ft. | Norway |
| Cuquenan | 2,000 ft. | Venezuela |
| Sutherland | 1,902 ft. | New Zealand |
| Kjellfossen | 1,840 ft. | Norway |

## Oceans

● The oceans make up 97 percent of the Earth's water.

● Most of an iceberg is hidden underwater. Only 10 percent of it floats above the surface.

● The greatest difference in tides is in the Bay of Fundy in Canada. The difference between low tide and high tide is about 54 ft. (16.5 m).

● The highest underwater mountain is in the ocean between Samoa and New Zealand. Its summit is 28,500 ft. (8,690 m) above the seabed.

● The White Sea, in Russia, has the lowest temperature, only 28°F (−2°C).

● The Persian Gulf is the warmest sea. In the summer its temperature reaches 96°F (35.6°C).

● The world's saltiest sea is the inland Dead Sea, in the Middle East.

## Coastlines

● The total length of all of Earth's coastlines is more than 310,700 miles (500,000 km) — the equivalent of over 12 times round the world.

● There are over 36 countries that do not have access to the open sea.

● Hudson's Bay in Canada is the largest bay in the world.

## Polar regions

● About 10 percent of all land on Earth is covered in ice.

● Icebergs can float at about 1.5 mph (2.5 km/h), with the help of a strong wind.

● The tallest iceberg ever seen measured 550 ft. (167.6 m) high. It was spotted near Greenland.

● On the tundra only one type of tree grows — the dwarf willow tree. It grows to a maximum height of 4 inches (10 cm).

● About 75 percent of all the fresh water on Earth is ice (ice-sheets and glaciers).

● People in Greenland live only on the coasts, because most of the country is covered in an ice sheet.

The ice sheet in Greenland:
● is 1 to 2 miles (1.5–3 km) thick.
● covers almost 0.5 million sq. miles (1.5 million sq. km).
● has an average temperature of −4°F (−20°C).

The Antarctic ice sheet:
● is 2 to 2½ miles (3–4 km) thick.
● covers 5 million sq. miles (13 million sq. km).
● has temperatures as low as −58°F (−50°C).

The Arctic Ocean:
● has about 4.5 million sq. miles (12 million sq. km) of floating ice.
● has an average depth of 5,000 ft. (1,500 m).
● has an average water temperature of −60°F (−51°C).
● There is no land at all at the North Pole, only ice on top of sea.
● There is six months of light followed by six months of darkness at the Poles.

## Deserts

● About 46,330 sq. miles (120,000 sq. km) of new desert is formed each year.

● Snow has been known to fall in the Sahara Desert.

Here are some of the world's largest deserts:

| Desert | Location | Area |
|---|---|---|
| Sahara | North Africa | 3,243,243 sq. mi. |
| Australian | Australia | 598,455 sq. mi. |
| Arabian | Middle East | 501,930 sq. mi. |
| Gobi | Mongolia/ China | 401,544 sq. mi. |
| Kalahari | Southern Africa | 200,772 sq. mi. |
| Takla Makan | China | 123,552 sq. mi. |
| Sonoran | USA/ Mexico | 119,691 sq. mi. |

● Only about 15 percent of the world's desert areas are sandy.

● Sand dunes can be as high as 1,300 ft. (400 m).

Here are some of the worst droughts in history:

| Year | Country | Estimated number of people killed |
|---|---|---|
| 1333–37 | China | over 4 million |
| 1769–70 | India | 3–10 million |
| 1837–38 | India | 800,000 |
| 1865–66 | India | 10 million |
| 1876–78 | India | 3.5 million |
| 1876–79 | China | 9–13 million |
| 1891–92 | Russia | 400,000 |
| 1892–94 | China | 1 million |
| 1896–97 | India | 5 million |
| 1899–1900 | India | 1 million |

## Weather

• Lightning travels at speeds of up to 930 miles (1,500 km) per second as it strikes down. It moves even faster as it travels back up again.

• The air in the path of lightning can reach temperatures of 54,000°F (30,000°C).

• A tornado can travel at 30 mph (50 km/h)

• The winds at the edge of a tornado spin fastest — more than 435 mph (700 km/h).

• Each year more than 16 million thunderstorms occur.

Here are some of the worst recent natural disasters:

• 1906 — A typhoon killed 50,000 people in Hong Kong.

• 1955 — In the U.S.A., 200 people were killed by a hurricane.

• 1962 — An avalanche in Peru killed 3,000 people.

• 1970 — In Bangladesh a cyclone and tidal waves killed 1 million people.

• 1975 — Lightning in Zimbabwe killed 21 people.

Here are some of the world's most rainy places:

• Mawsynram in India has an annual rainfall of 470 inches (11,873 mm).

• Tutunendo in Colombia is slightly drier with 460 inches (11,770 mm) a year.

• Cherrapunji in India has an annual rainfall of 450 inches (11,430 mm)

## Plant life

• The largest tree in the world is a giant sequoia growing in California. It is nearly 275 ft. (84 m) tall and measures 83 ft. (25.3 m) round the trunk.

• The fastest-growing tree is the eucalyptus. It can grow 33 ft. (10 m) a year.

• The world's oldest trees are the bristlecone pines of California. One of them is about 4,700 years old.

• The largest flower comes from the rafflesia plant. The flower can weigh 15 pounds (7 kg) and grow to a width of 3 ft. (91 cm).

Here are some of the most heavily forested countries:

| Country | % of country's total area covered by forest |
|---|---|
| Surinam | 92 |
| Solomon Islands | 91 |
| Papua New Guinea | 84 |
| Guyana | 83 |
| French Guiana | 82 |
| Gabon | 78 |
| Finland | 76 |
| Cambodia | 75 |
| North Korea | 74 |
| Bhutan | 70 |

• The tallest type of grass is bamboo. It can grow up to about 100 ft. (30 m) high.

• The saguaro is the tallest kind of cactus. It can grow to about 52 ft. (16 m) high.

Here are some different types of cereal:

• Barley
• Maize
• Millet
• Oats
• Rice
• Rye
• Wheat

Here are six types of coniferous trees (i.e. they produce cones):

• Cedar
• Cypress
• Douglas fir
• Larch
• Pine
• Spruce

## Forests

• Some medicines are made from forest trees. For instance, quinine, which is used to treat malaria, comes originally from a chemical found in the bark of the cinchona tree.

• Only 1 percent of sunlight reaches the rainforest floor.

Here are six types of deciduous trees (i.e. they lose their leaves in the fall):

• Ash
• Birch
• Chestnut
• Elm
• Maple
• Oak

• Lianas are strong ropelike rain forest plants. They can grow to a width of 6 ft. (2 m) and are strong enough to swing on.

• The largest forest in the world covers parts of Scandinavia and northern Russia and has a total area of over 3.5 million sq. miles (9 million sq. km).

## Saving the Earth

• In 1952 about 4,000 people died in London, England from air pollution.

• 90 million tons of sulfur dioxide was released globally per year in the 1980s. 22 million tons of this was contributed by the U.S.A.

• Over 4 million cars in Brazil are now running on gasohol. Gasohol is made from sugar cane and causes much less air pollution than gasoline.

# INDEX